Wake Up & Taste The Coffee

Secrets to Stay Awake and Elevate the Taste of Coffee

Ryan Reddick

Copyright © 2023 Ryan Reddick

All rights reserved.

ISBN: 979-8-9885646-5-2

Wake Up & Taste The Coffee

Secrets to stay awake and elevate the taste of Coffee © Copyright by Rosie B, Book Publishing LLC

ISBN 979-8-9885646-2-1 (Audio)
ISBN 979-8-9885646-5-2 (Hardback)
ISBN 979-8-9885646-1-4 (eBook)

All rights reserved

The content within this book may not be reproduced, duplicated or transmitted without direct written permission from the author or the publisher.
Under no circumstances will any blame or legal responsibility be held against the publisher, or author, for any damages, reparation, or monetary loss due to the information within this book, either directly or indirectly.

Legal Notice

This book is copyright protected. It is only for personal use. You cannot amend, distribute, sell, use, quote or paraphrase any part or the content within this book without the consent of the author or publisher.

Disclaimer Notice

Please note the information within this document is for educational and entertainment purposes only. All effort has been executed to present correct, up-to-date, reliable, and complete information. No warranties of any kind are declared or implied.

Readers acknowledge that the author is not engaged in rendering legal, financial, medical, or professional advice. The content within this book has been derived from various sources. Please consult a licensed professional before attempting any techniques outlined in this book.

By reading this document, the reader agrees that under no circumstances is the author responsible for any losses, direct or indirect, that are incurred because of the use of the information within this document, including, but not limited to, errors, omissions, or inaccuracies.

Book cover Design by @elhaqfarid

Book Editing by @samwrightwrites

Published by Rosie B, Book Publishing LLC Ewa Beach, HI 96706

DEDICATION

I dedicate this book to my lovely wife, Judith, my aunt, Patty, Robin, my dear mother, Peggy, and all my friends and family.

Table Of Contents

____ *01*

How to brew the best cup of coffee that will change your life:

____ *05*

Secrets and special techniques to master the brewing process:

____ *09*

Create the perfect cup that wakes you up:

____ *14*

Fun Recipes

ACKNOWLEDGMENTS

Thank you for taking the time to read this Book. Before we look into reading "Wake Up & Taste The Coffee" you should understand how important it is to elevate your coffee. My approach has been tested with great success that has helped many people I've encountered. I apply this skill and technique every day, and it works. My energy levels have increased, and my coffee is more delicious. This is my story, so now I challenge you.

How To Brew The Best Cup Of Coffee That Will Change Your Life:

What Is Brewing Coffee?

Brewing coffee uses water to extract taste and aroma from ground coffee beans. Many brewing techniques include cold brew, pour-over, espresso, and drip brewing. The flavor and aroma of the final cup of coffee can be affected by the water's quality, the coffee– to - water ratio, and the coffee beans' grind size.

Different methods may take slightly different procedures, but they all require combining the coffee and water in a precise way, depending on the equipment and technique that we use, brewing coffee can be a simple or complex process. However, with practice and experimentation, you can find the best method and consistently enjoy a good cup of coffee.

The Importance Of Water Quality

Water quality is an important factor in brewing coffee, as it can affect the taste, aroma, extraction, and performance of the coffee brewing equipment. To ensure the best cup of coffee, it is important to use high-quality water with a TDS reading of 150-300 ppm (parts per million). Paying attention to water quality can enhance the coffee's flavor, aroma, and overall enjoyment.

Choosing The Right Coffee Beans

Choosing the right coffee beans for brewing is essential to creating a delicious cup of coffee. Factors to consider include roast level, origin, variety, freshness, and fair trade and organic. Experiment and try different varieties until you find the one you enjoy the most.

Grind Size And Its Impact On Taste

The grind size of coffee beans can significantly impact the taste of brewed coffee. It affects extraction, strength, acidity, and bitterness. To determine the best grind size for your coffee brewing method, experiment with different grind sizes until you find the one that produces a flavor profile you can enjoy. By paying attention to the grind size, finer grounds can result in a more bitter cup of coffee.

Measuring Coffee

Measuring coffee for brewing is an important step that affects the flavor and strength of the final cup. There are three ways to measure coffee: a digital scale, a coffee scoop, and a measuring cup. Pre-ground coffee should be followed by the manufacturer's instructions. Experiment with different ratios and amounts of coffee until you find the perfect balance for your taste.

Secrets and special technique to master the brewing process:

French press and pour-over are the best brewing methods that maximize flavor and provide full caffeine.

French Press

Pour Over

A French press is a coffee brewing device that uses immersion brewing to produce full-bodied and rich coffee. It comprises a cylindrical glass or stainless-steel container with a plunger and a metal or nylon mesh filter.

Pour-over coffee is a coffee brewing method that involves pouring hot water over coffee grounds in a filter. It is known for its clean and bright taste and can be made with different types of filters and a gooseneck kettle. It is popular in specialty coffee shops and home brewing. Pour the brewed coffee into a mug and enjoy!

French Press

How To Brew:

First, bring water to a boil. A standard 1- liter French press requires 500ml of water, and the temp must be 90-95°C. While the water is boiling, grind your coffee beans about 60 grams. Try to grind your coffee beans slightly more coarsely than table salt.

Add the ground coffee to the French press. After boiling the water, pour it over the coffee grounds in the French press.

Stir gently with a spoon or paddle to ensure all the coffee grounds are fully immersed in the water.

Place the plunger on top of the French press but do not press it down yet. Let the coffee steep for 4-5 minutes.

After 4-5 minutes, slowly press the plunger down to separate the coffee grounds from the liquid coffee.

Pour Over

First, bring water to a boil. For a standard pour-over, you will need about 300 ml of water, and the temp must be 90-95°C.

While the water is boiling, grind your coffee beans about 20 grams for a single cup pour-over, and try to grind medium fine.

Place a paper filter in the pour-over dripper and rinse it with hot water to remove any paper taste and preheat the dripper.

Add the ground coffee to the filter. Pour 40 ml of hot water over ground coffee and let the coffee bloom for 30 sec.

After 30 sec, slowly pour the remaining hot water over the coffee grounds in a circular motion. This process should take about 2-3 minutes.

Remove the dripper and filter after the coffee has finished dripping and pour the coffee into a mug. Enjoy your tasty pour-over coffee!

Create The Perfect Cup That Wakes You Up:

Creating the perfect cup of coffee involves several factors that work together to produce a delicious and satisfying cup.

How To Adjust Brewing Parameters To Achieve The Desired Taste

Changing the brewing parameters may help achieve an ideal flavor profile in coffee.

These parameters include coffee-to-water ratio, grind size, water temperature, brewing time, and water quality. Adjusting the coffee-to-water ratio will result in a stronger and more flavorful cup, while a lower ratio will produce a milder taste. Changing the grind size will affect the extraction of the coffee, while water temperature can affect the extraction level and the coffee's strength and flavor. Brewing time is also important, with longer brewing times producing a stronger and more intense flavor, while shorter brewing times produce a milder taste.

Water quality can also affect the taste of the coffee, with filtered or purified water removing any impurities or off-flavors. Experimenting with different parameters and combinations can result in a wide range of taste profiles, letting coffee lovers find their perfect cup.

Different Brewing Techniques Make Unique Flavor Profiles

Various brewing techniques are an excellent way to create unique flavor profiles in coffee. Different brewing methods produce different extraction levels, which can affect the flavor and strength of the coffee.

For example, French press coffee requires a longer steeping time, which can result in a strong and intense flavor.

But pour-over coffee requires less time to brew, giving it a smoother and cleaner flavor. A lighter and more delicate flavor results from the paper filter's function to filtrate the majority of the coffee oils and sediment.

Another example is the AeroPress, which combines drip and immersion brewing elements. It produces a quick and clean flavor by applying pressure to extract the coffee flavors quickly.

By experimenting with different brewing techniques, coffee lovers can create a customized cup of coffee tailored to their individual tastes and preferences.

Choose The Right Roast Beans

There are many roasts, some of which are lighter roasts like City or Cinnamon roasts roasted for a shorter period and at a lower temperature to bring out the natural flavors of the coffee bean. When medium roasts, like FullCity or American roast, are roasted longer and at a higher temperature, the resulting flavor profile is more even and complex. And for dark roasts, such as French or Italian roasts, are roasted for the longest time and at the highest temperature, producing a bolder and more robust flavor profile.

Choosing the right roast for your taste involves considering several factors, including the coffee bean, the roast level, and your taste. The coffee bean plays an essential role in determining the flavor profile of your coffee, while the roast level can significantly affect its flavor. Darker roasts are typically associated with bolder, more intense flavors, while lighter roasts have more subtle and nuanced flavors. Experiment with different roast levels to find the one that best suits your taste. Trusting your taste buds is essential when choosing the right roast. Overall, choosing the right roast for your taste involves considering various factors and experimenting with different roasts until you find the one that satisfies your palate.

NEED MORE INSIGHT?

Here Are Some Coffee Recipes

Cold Brew

Cold brew is a refreshing alternative to traditional iced coffee that involves steeping coarsely ground coffee beans in cold or room-temperature water for an extended period, typically 12–24 hours.

Ingredients

50 g Coffee Beans

Instruction

1. First, grind coffee beans coarsely.
2. In a jar or container, combine ground coffee and water.
3. Give it a gentle stir to make sure all the grounds are saturated. Cover the container and place it in the fridge.
4. Let it steep for 12–24 hours.
5. Once the steeping time is over, strain the coffee using cheesecloth to remove the grounds.
6. Serve in a glass and enjoy!

Espresso

Espresso is a concentrated coffee beverage made by pressing hot water through finely-ground coffee beans.

Ingredients

19 g Coffee Beans

Instruction

1. First, grind the coffee beans finely and put them into a portafilter.
2. Preheat the espresso machine by running hot water through the group head.
3. Tamp the coffee grounds into the basket of your portafilter with a tamper to make sure the grounds are evenly distributed and tightly packed.
4. Before putting it in the group head, wipe off any excess coffee grounds from the rim of the portafilter, then insert it into the espresso machine's group head and lock it tight.
5. Place a shot glass under the spout of the portafilter to catch the espresso as it is brewed. Start the espresso machine and let it brew until 38 ml for a double shot. This typically takes about 25-30 seconds.
6. Once the espresso is brewed, remove the portafilter from the machine and knock out the used coffee grounds into a knock box.
7. Enjoy the fresh espresso or you can use it as a base for other espresso-based drinks.

Vanilla Latte

A vanilla latte is a sweet, creamy coffee drink with vanilla syrup, steamed milk, and a shot of espresso.

Ingredients

Single Shot Espresso

15 ml Vanilla Syrup

150 ml Fresh Milk

Instruction

1. Brew a good espresso into a latte glass.
2. After brewing an espresso, pour vanilla syrup over espresso.
3. Swirl the glass to combine and break the crema of the espresso.
4. Heat and froth milk using a steam wand attached to the espresso machine. The milk should be heated to around 65–70 °C, or your palm can't handle the heat. Frothed milk should have a velvety texture.
5. Pour frothed milk over the mix. Serve and enjoy!

Hazelnut Latte

A hazelnut latte is a sweet, creamy coffee drink with hazelnut syrup, steamed milk, and an espresso shot.

Ingredients

Single Shot Espresso
15 ml Vanilla Syrup
150 ml Fresh Milk

Instruction

1. Brew a good espresso into a latte glass.
2. After brewing an espresso, pour hazelnut syrup over the espresso. Swirl the glass to combine and break the crema of the espresso.
3. Heat and froth milk using a steam wand attached to the espresso machine. The milk should be heated to around 65–70 °C, or your palm can't handle the heat. Frothed milk should have a velvety texture.
4. Pour frothed milk over the mix. Serve and enjoy!

Banana Coffee

A banana coffee is a sweet, creamy, and refreshing drink made with coffee, milk, ice, and banana flavoring.

Ingredients

Single Shot Espresso

19g Banana Frappe Powder or a Whole Banana Fruit

15 ml Vanilla Syrup

120 ml Fresh Milk Whipped Cream

Ice Cubes

Instruction

1. Brew a good espresso into a shot glass. Combine all ingredients in the blender.
2. Blend the ingredients until they are smooth and creamy. You can add more ice or milk as needed to adjust the thickness and texture of the frappe.
3. Pour the blended drink into a tall glass and garnish with whipped cream and some banana slices. Serve and enjoy!

Raspberry White Choco Coffee

A raspberry white Choco is a rich and creamy coffee-based beverage made with coffee, milk, ice, and some flavoring.

Ingredients

Single Shot Espresso
10 g Cream Cheese
15 ml White Chocolate Syrup
15 ml Raspberry Syrup
120 ml Fresh Milk
Whipped Cream
Ice Cubes

Instruction

1. Brew a good espresso into a shot glass. Combine all ingredients in the blender.
2. Blend the ingredients until they are smooth and creamy. You can add more ice or milk as needed to adjust the thickness and texture of the frappe.
3. Pour the blended drink into a tall glass and garnish with whipped cream and cocoa powder. Serve and enjoy!

Black Forest Coffee

A black forest coffee drink is typically inspired by a black forest cake.

Ingredients

Double Shot Espresso

20 g Chocolate Frappe Powder

15 ml Rum Syrup

15 ml Vanilla Syrup

120 ml Fresh Milk

Whipped Cream

Ice Cubes

Instruction

1. Brew a good espresso into a shot glass. Combine all ingredients in the blender.
2. Blend the ingredients until they are smooth and creamy. You can add more ice or milk as needed to adjust the thickness and texture of the frappe.
3. Pour the blended drink into a tall glass and garnish with whipped cream and chocolate sauce. Serve and enjoy!

Spice Latte

A spice latte is a type of coffee-based beverage that typically has a combination of warm spices and milk.

Ingredients

Singles Shot Espresso

20 ml Homemade Spice Syrup

50 ml Fresh Milk

Ice Cubes

Ingredients Syrup

1 cup Granulated Sugar

1 cup Water

1 Stick Cinnamon

½ tsp Whole Clove

½ tsp Whole Cardamom

¼ tsp Ground Ginger

Instruction

1. Brew a good espresso into a shot glass.
2. After brewing an espresso, pour homemade syrup, add ice cubes into the glass.
3. Pour fresh milk and stir gently.
4. Pour espresso on top of the milk.

How to make spice syrup

- Over medium heat, put the sugar and water in a medium saucepan.
- Stir the mixture until the sugar is completely dissolved.
- After that, Add all spices to the saucepan. Stir the mixture to combine.
- Bring the mixture to a boil, then reduce to a low heat and continue to cook for 15-20 minutes.
- Remove the saucepan from the heat and let it cool.

After the liquid has cooled, pour it into a clean jar or bottle using a fine-mesh strainer.

- Store the syrup in the refrigerator for up to one month.

Hazelnut Mocha

Hazelnut mocha is a type of coffee-based beverage that combines the rich flavors of mocha with the nutty and sweet taste of hazelnuts.

Ingredients

Double Shot Espresso
20 g Chocolate powder
15 ml Hazelnut Syrup
150 ml Fresh Milk
Ice Cubes

Instruction

1. Brew a good espresso into a shot glass.
2. Add espresso, chocolate powder, and hazelnut syrup to the glass.
3. Stir until it dissolves and add an ice cube.
4. Pour fresh milk over the mix.
5. Serve and enjoy!

Cold Brew Spritzer

A cold brew spritzer is a refreshing and fizzy drink that combines cold brew coffee with sparkling water.

Ingredients

60 ml Cold Brew
80 ml Sparkling water
15 ml Lemon Juice
20 ml Peach Syrup
Ice Cubes

Instruction

1. First, squeeze fresh lemon juice into the glass, then add syrup and cold brew. Stir gently to combine.
2. Add ice cubes to the mix.
3. Finish with sparkling water.
4. Serve and enjoy!

White Cold Brew

White cold brew is inspired by a white Russian cocktail with a sweet and creamy taste.

Ingredients

100 ml Cold Brew

15 ml Rum Syrup

15 ml Vanilla Syrup

25 ml Whipped Cream

25 ml Fresh Milk

Ice Cubes

Instruction

1. First, combine vanilla syrup, whipped cream, and fresh milk in a large mixing bowl. After combining, froth until it's frothy.
2. Fill a rock glass with ice.
3. Pour rum syrup and cold brew into the glass.
4. Stir gently to combine.
5. Slowly pour cream over the top of the liquid.
6. Serve and enjoy!

Note: You can froth the mixture using a hand mixer at low speed, or by hand using a wire whisk. Wire whisk is recommended.

Lemonade Cherry Coffee

Lemonade cherry coffee is a refreshing and fruity coffee-based beverage that combines the flavors of lemonade, cherry syrup, and coffee.

Ingredients

Single Shot Espresso

10 ml Orange Syrup

20 ml Cherry Syrup

120 ml Lemon-lime Soda

Ice Cubes

Instruction

1. Brew a good espresso into a shot glass. Pour syrup into the glass.
2. Add ice cubes and lemon-lime soda.
3. Stir gently to combine.
4. Slowly pour espresso on the top of the mix. Serve and enjoy!

Measurements Conversion Chart

Dry Measurements

Measurements	Equivalent
1 Lb	16 ounces
1 cup	16 Tbsp
3/4 cup	12 Tbsp
2/3 cup	10 Tbsp plus 2 tsp
1/2 cup	8 Tbsp
3/8 cup	6 Tbsp
1/3 cup	5 Tbsp plus 1 tsp
1/4 cup	4 Tbsp
1/6 cup	2 Tbsp plus 2 tsp
1/8 cup	2 Tbsp
1/16 cup	1 Tbsp
1 Tbsp	3 tsp
1/8 tsp	Pinch
1/16 tsp	Dash
1/2 cup butter	1 stick of butter

Liquid Measurements

Measurements	Equivalent
4 quarts	1 gallon
2 quarts	1/2 gallon
1 quart	1/4 gallon
2 pints	1 quart
4 cups	1 quart
2 cups	1/2 quart
2 cups	1 pint
1 cup	1/2 pint
1 cup	1/4 quart
1 cup	8 fluid ounces
3/4 cup	6 fluid ounces
2/3 cup	5.3 fluid ounces
1/2 cup	4 fluid ounces
1/3 cup	2.7 fluid ounces
1/4 cup	2 fluid ounces
1 Tbsp	0.5 fluid ounces

U.S. to Metric Conversions

Weight Measurements	Metric Conversion
1 Lb	454 grams
8 ounces	227 grams
4 ounces	113 grams
1 ounce	28 grams
Volume Measurements	
4 quarts	3.8 liters
4 cups (1 quart)	0.95 liters
2 cups	473 milliliters
1 cup	237 milliliters
3/4 cup	177 milliliters
2/3 cup	158 milliliters
1/2 cup	118 milliliters
1/3 cup	79 milliliters
1/4 cup	59 milliliters
1/5 cup	47 milliliters
1 Tbsp	15 milliliters
1 tsp	5 milliliters
1/2 tsp	2.5 milliliters
1/5 tsp	1 milliliter
Fluid Measurements	
34 fluid ounces	1 liter
8 fluid ounces	237 milliliters
3.4 fluid ounces	100 milliliters
1 fluid ounce	30 milliliters

Oven Temperatures

250°F	120°C
320°F	160°C
350°F	180°C
400°F	205°C
425°F	220°C

CONCLUSION

The art of coffee brewing is a complex and rewarding skill that requires knowledge, practice, and creativity. By understanding the key factors influencing the flavor and quality of coffee, such as bean origin, roast level, water temperature, and brewing method, you can create a delicious and satisfying cup of coffee that reflects your preferences and style. With a willingness to experiment, learn, and refine your methods, you can elevate your coffee experience and discover the true pleasure of a perfectly brewed cup of coffee.

ABOUT THE AUTHOR

Ryan Reddick, A coffee connoisseur who innovates fresh new ideas and recipes of coffee. He educates on how to properly prepare coffee in fascinating new ways. Ryan is married and resides in Hawaii. He has cooked in many restaurants and has the gift of enhancing food flavors. His great-grandmother Rosie B. Johnson inspired him to learn how to prepare delicious coffee.

www.ingramcontent.com/pod-product-compliance
Lightning Source LLC
Chambersburg PA
CBHW051328110526
44582CB00003B/84